GW01085832

Windows 10:

2020 User Guide to Master Your
Personal Computer with 33
Windows Hidden features.

ISBN: 9798639218255

CONTENTS

Introduction

Windows 10 is the latest in the succession of the operating systems developed by Microsoft. The operating system became obtainable to the public on July 29 in the year 2015. It has various attributes, which makes using it an enticing experience. It updates regularly and comes at zero cost. You can describe the operating system as a service that receives updates to its attributes and enhance enterprise environments to receive updates at a slow pace. It has a compatibility with universal apps and also functions properly with touch-screen applications within the OS 8. The operating system 10 also comes with a new browser called Microsoft Edge web browser that lets users log in with the use of the face. It supports biometric validation, task view, and some security problems for work surroundings, which is an improvement when you compare it to other versions. Users can also benefit from the assistance of Cortana on the operating system 10.

Chapter 1 – What is Windows 10

The operating system 10 is the most recent version and part of the Microsoft family. The manufacturers announced the introduction of the operating system at a press conference in the year 2014 and were available for personal computers on July 29, 2015. It started as a free upgrade to users utilizing the operating system 7 and 8.1 for a year. The operating system provides a straightforward and easy to use user interface for different systems such as laptop, desktop, tablets, intelligent mobiles, and games console. It helps Microsoft with the integration on each of those platforms without discomfort.

The operating system comes with enhanced biometric support for authorization via the Hello platform for Windows. Gadgets with supported cameras allow users to log into the device via the use of facial recognition. Gadgets with supported readers let users log in with the use of fingerprints.

The Windows 10 gets regular updates with new attributes depending on the feedback provided by users. The manufacturing company provides updates every six months, and updates can include software and programs update. Every release consists of the four-digit build (a version number), and the first two number refers to the release year of the operating system, and the last two indicates the month of release. The operating system functions properly with universal Windows platforms. The applications run across different platforms and gadget classes, which include tablets Xbox console, intelligent mobies, and other devices compatible with the operating system gadgets. Windows applications can share codes on different platforms and have designs that are responsive and can adapt to the device requirements and available inputs. The operating system also synchronizes data from one Windows 10 gadget to another, information like notifications, or play games on a cross-platform, credentials, and so on.

Chapter 2 – The difference between Windows 7/8/XP/Vista to Windows 10

Lots of people prefer upgrading to the operating system 10 from Windows 7,8, XP, or vista to avoid loss of data instead of installing it from scratch. It is a simple task to perform, but you need to follow instructions for seamless upgrading or installation.

What you need to upgrade to the operating system 10

If you want to upgrade systems to Windows 10, there are few things that you require and also a little practice to safeguard your information and get the installation concept of the operating system. Before you perform any task, ensure that you have an activated Windows version. If your version is a pirated one, you cannot complete an upgrade or installation. To know if you have the right Windows version, follow the below method:

Hold the Windows + W control key

together to launch settings

Input "Activate" into the search field

Examine and see if it activates successfully.

Another method to perform that task is to launch the control panel menu and go to the System section, and you will see if you have the correct installation or not.

If you run the operating system 7, right-click "My Computer" and select properties, and you will see if you have the installation beneath the displayed options. You will see if you have an activated version or not.

Back up the device

Backing up devices should be a regular

exercise for every computer user. You should ensure that you completely back up the device because if the installation fails and you have to go back to your previous version, your data will be safe and protected.

Uninstall or deactivate Anti-virus Software

Lots of antiviruses get in the way of installation with little or no reason. Users should turn off any antivirus on the device before starting the upgrade process. You can install the antivirus or turn it back on when you complete the process.

Get the operating system 10 Update Assistant

You should download the operating system update assistant. You can get the assistant on the manufacturing company's official website, and users can download it for 64-bit or 32-bit. The tool helps to automatically identify your computer version and get the right operating system files.

When you download the files, you can now run the installer. The computer will ask you to upgrade now, do that, and move to the next stage.

Go through the license terms and click accept to begin the installation. Now, select install to get the operating system on your personal computer.

The set will demand your preferences, and you can continue to click on them to move further. When you complete the installation, you can enjoy the experience and advantages of the operating system.

The difference between the operating system 10, XP, 8, and 7

Cost: While users that run the OS 7, XP, Vista and 8 will not get the most recent version for free, but when it comes to upgrading, it comes at zero cost, you do not have to pay anything for upgrading.

Extended Support: A critical reason for users to get the most recent version is that it has the extended and mainstream support of Microsoft much longer than the OS 7 and 8.

The mainstream support is the function and attributes limit, which makes it less critical, but extended support is when the manufacturing company continues to provide security updates. OS 10 offers extended five-year support over the operating system 7 and an additional two to OS 8.

Universal Applications and flexibility- OS 10 can function properly across all future gadgets from the manufacturing company, which includes desktops and intelligent mobiles and lots more.

Game- The OS 10 consist of the DirectX 12, which is a must-have for gamers. It offers 30-40% of enhanced performance over the DX11 that you will find in previous versions. OS 7 and 8 do not have access to the DX12. The OS 10 also supports game streaming through an Xbox one. The device controllers have great compatibility with personal computers that run on it. Users can now play different games on personal laptops or desktop in a few minutes. The game streaming is responsive and very fast, it is a feature that you will not find on the OS 7, 8, XP, and vista at a later date.

Cortana/search- The OS 8 provides an excellent online search within its Start menu, and it only offers local searches, it can search for items on the same computer, but that is not the case on the OS 10. The reason is that Cortana has similar functions to the voice search on Andriod or Siri on iOS. The tool gives replies to speech commands and executes every task given to it, starting from searching the internet to important tasks across the operating system 10 like calendar entries and lots more. The tool is not a perfect one but functions excellently and will improve overtime.

Virtual desktop and Edge Browser- The operating system 10 comes with the Edge browser, which is the manufacturing company's attempt to topple Chrome. The browser functions faster than the internet explorer that you will find on the operating system XP, Vista, 7, and 8. You can find the browser only on the operating system 10.

It also includes Virtual Desktops similar to the ones you will find in Mac operating systems and Linux. The desktops allow users without setting up various virtual desktops that you can use for work or other exercises. It is an excellent attribute.

Security - While the OS 7, Vista, XP, and 8 perform an excellent job in securing users, the OS 10 comes with an enhanced game with different interesting attributes. The first feature is the gadget guard that blocks attacks coming from unsigned software applications and programs. The feature also functions virtually and can also neutralize software that can affect the computer system.

Chapter 3 – Windows 10 installation and its first setup

You have to be excited about the new attributes of the operating system 10, which includes the Cortana, Edge browser, action center, and so on. The process of installing Windows 10 is an easy one compared to all of the previous versions. To perform a clean installation and setup of the operating system 10 on your personal computer, follow the following steps:

1. Firstly, download the operating system 10 ISO file from the operating system page on the Microsoft page.

2. After downloading the file, send the file to the installation media like DVD or the universal serial bus flash drive. With this step, you will develop a loadable operating system 10 flash drive. When the loadable flash is ready, the Windows installation can begin on your personal computer whenever you want. What you need to do is to connect the loadable flash to the computer and follow the below steps.

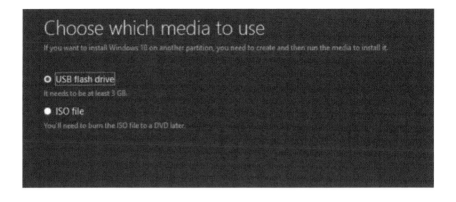

3. Proceed to the medial installation and double-tap the setup.exe to load.

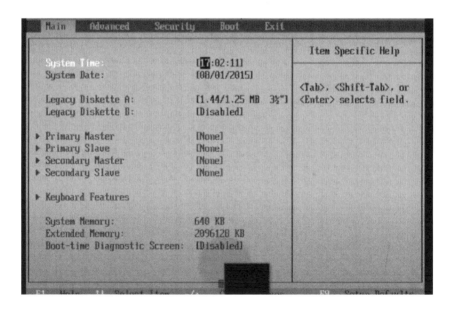

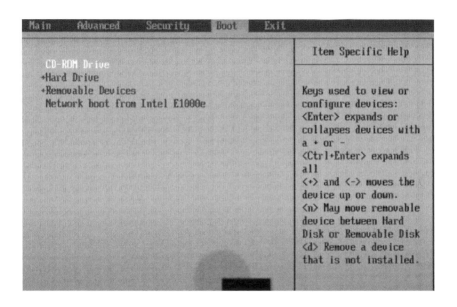

4. Choose your preferred language, keyboard, and format and select next.

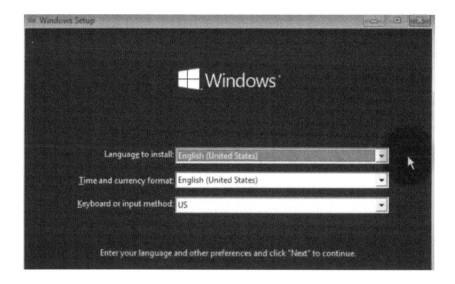

5. When you get to the visual display that shows install now, select the install button to begin.

6. Select ok on the license term and select next.

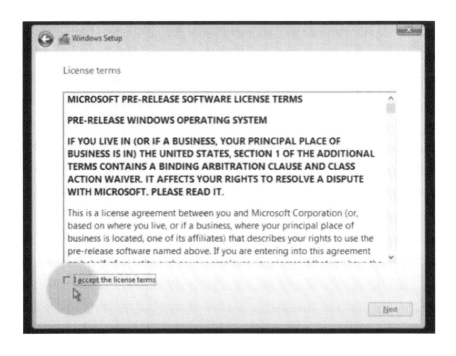

7. The following screen will show two options asking you the type of installation you prefer.

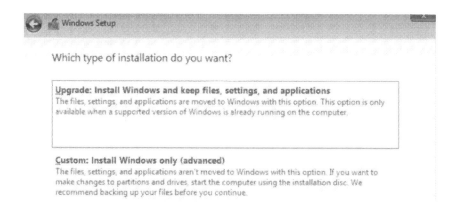

In a few cases, you might have a window installation that exists already and does not want to lose your files, settings, and apps, select the option for upgrade. If the operating system does not support the Windows version that exists, or you want a clean installation, then you should select the custom option.

8. If you choose the option to upgrade, you should skip this step. But if you utilize the custom installation, choose Windows partition on the point you

want the operating system 10 to be installed and select next.

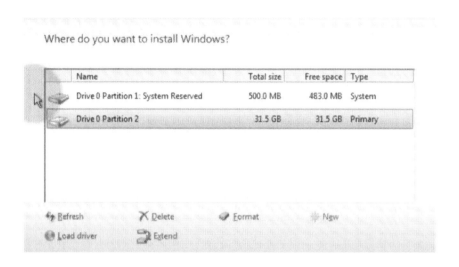

9. Now the operating system 10 installations will begin. You have to be patient now till all the Windows updates complete.

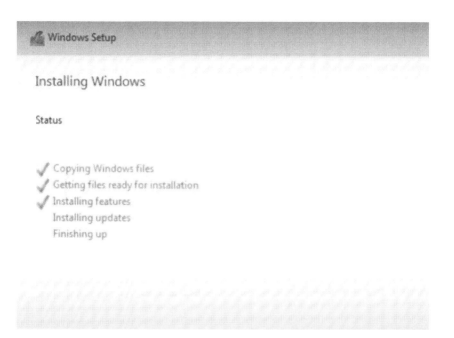

10.   After getting the Windows updates installed, your personal computer will reload in fifteen seconds. Select the restart button to restart the personal computer.

11. When the computer restarts, notifications such as getting the computer ready will display, and it

begins to display its percentage as it progresses.

12. The computer will then restart again.

13. Proceed to the settings screen, and select utilize specific settings control key to keep default settings on the computer or select the customize control key to modify default settings.

14. When you select the customize control key, it will display the screen for settings. On that screen, adjust the changes to your preferred choice and select next.

15. Input your password and username and select the finish.

16. Now the settings will complete itself.

17. You can now see animations with several colors on the pc screen, and you need to wait till it installs completely.

18. Now you are done with the installation and setup process, and the exciting experience can begin.

Chapter 4 – Windows 10 applications and programs

The Microsoft Store consists of different selection of great apps that users can utilize for lots of different things. You will find lots of simple applications to apps that can enhance productivity.

However, below are a few applications that you can use on your personal computer or tablet running on the operating system 10.

Dropbox

It is an outstanding service that can host lots of files. It is a storage service that functions as a modern workspace because it lets users remain connected to the team and have access directly to files stored in a location. If you and your team need to share large files, or you need to free-up spaces on your gadget, the application has lots of different apps and have a simple and straightforward user interface. It is an app that is best at storing documents and functions excellently with the OS 10.

VLC

The popular media player application is also obtainable as an application on the OS 10. It has a better design and looks compared to the version that you use on desktop computers. The application has different video formats compatibility, which includes mp4, avi, and the likes. The application also comes with lots of extra attributes like the video and audio sync, utilizing videos as live wallpapers, adding subtitles, and so on. It is a great media player app that is compatible with OS 10 gadgets, and users will love this one when it comes to music and video playing.

Amazon Music

It is a wonderful music application that subscribed users can use to stream via Amazon Prime. The app gives users access to over two million songs without any advert disturbance. Users can also download music offline as well as get free skips. They are the attributes reserved for paid subscribers of other platforms for streaming, such as Spotify and so on. It also offers music selection that is lesser than what you will get on Spotify, which can be over thirty million music. It is hard to miss a song on this platform. It is a wonderful application for the lovers of music who want to enjoy the music of their choice at zero cost. The service also offers a free service that offers the user a music collection of over fifty million.

Audible

The application is for book lovers, and if you are a fan of books, then you should not miss out on this application. It is an audiobook platform that plays music to users on the go. The app allows users to have access to books while on a journey or performing chores in the house. Audible is one of the best application that you will find for reading books and has perfect compatibility with devices that run on the OS 10. If you are a book lover, then you should install the application. It has a straightforward user interface and realizes the user.

Reading Trainer

It is another wonderful application for learning, and it is an excellent app for kids to learn. It enhances the retention rate and speed of reading in kids with different fun exercises. You can also double the speed of your reading in two training days. However, you can perform that task if you want to read a large file in very little time. The exercises that the eyes go through play an important role in enhancing users' reading speed. The app is also compatible with devices that run on the OS 10.

How to work with files in Windows 10

Repair programs and applications: One of the most amazing things to do on the new operating system 10 is the repairing of programs and applications that do not function properly. However, you should know that options like repair or modifications will not be available for every program or app.

Repair options via the Settings page

Tap the start control key, then select settings > Apps > features and applications.

Choose the application that needs fixing.

Tap the link of advanced options below the application name (unavailable on some apps). On the following page, tap Repair if you can find the repair option. If repair is unavailable, then click on reset.

Repair options via Control Panel

Type Control Panel inside the search box and click it in results, then tap programs, attributes, and programs.

Perform a right-click on the program that needs fixing and tap repair, but if repair is unavailable, click on change. Then follow the on-screen prompts.

Uninstall programs and applications

There are several methods to uninstall programs and applications, so if one does not work for you, then you should try another. However, you should know that few applications developed by Windows that you cannot delete.

Uninstall via Start menu

Click on the start control key and find the app within the displayed list.

Right-click the program and click Uninstall.

Uninstall via the Settings page

Click on the start control key and tap settings > Apps > Attributes and applications.

Tap the application you want to perform the action on and uninstall.

Determine file system authorizations for all applications

On the other hand, you can also deny or give applications full entry into files, videos, pictures, and so on.

To control the file authorization, perform these tasks:

Launch Settings.

Tap Privacy.

Tap File System.

Feel free to control file access on the page in various methods.

For instance, to stop owners from choosing if their application will get entry into their documents, below the "give authorization to the file system" segment, Tap it and switch the file access off. To authorize or disallow all applications authorization into your files just on your account, then below the "give apps entry to your file system," switch it off. To authorize or deny comprehensive authorization to programs independently, below the "Choose apps that can gain entry into your file system" segment, switch it on or off for the programs you wish to authorize or disallow.

Fix default programs

There are several files of non-identical types on your personal computer. With Windows, it is straightforward to launch files by creating a default program for every kind of file, which includes picture files.

But if you do not like the operating system 10's default program or one of your installed apps creates a default program automatically, and you would like to reverse it. You should proceed to the settings to modify the application for contrasting protocols and file.

1. To modify applications for protocols and files, launch settings > System > Default applications.

2. You can modify applications for your map, email, calendar, and so on. Tap the existing default application, and you will get a pop-up with different applications you can utilize or a link somewhere. If you cannot find the needed application, proceed to the control panel to fix the app to default.

3. To fix independent files to default (e.g., as an alternative to utilizing one app to launch every picture file, you wish to utilize non-identical apps to launch files like PNGs and so on), tap select default applications through the file type. Search for the type of file and convert it to the default application, tap the existing default application, and pick the application to utilize from the pop-up.

4. To fix defaults for independent protocols (set up your personal

computer so that you Google mail account launches anytime you tap an email address while browsing), tap select default applications through the protocol. Search for the protocol you wish to modify the default application for, tap the existing default application, and tap the application you wish to utilize from the pop-up.

5. If you cannot find your desired application within the settings, proceed to your control panel. Tap fix default application to launch the control panel window of the fixed default applications. Search for your desired application and tap it. Tap fix the app as default for every protocol and type of file it can open.

Chapter 5 – Tips to protect your computer

The internet is part of our lives and daily routines, and we use the computer system to keep lots of vital information, and the system can become vulnerable to attacks in the online world. For that reason, users need to protect the device and information from malicious attacks. Below are few safeguarding measures to take for users to prevent the computer system running on OS 10 from damage, and risk.

Update the OS 10 software

One critical exercise to execute firstly is to secure your system and keep it safe from harm by updating the OS 10 programs. The manufacturing company continues to support the OS with recent updates for security measures to protect it from malicious attackers. However, the OS 10 get updates and install them, and users can also ensure that the computer has the most recent patches installed on it. Proceed to settings, select security, and update, and check for updates control by clicking its control key.

Upgrade to the most recent version of the OS

Because you run the OS 10 does not mean that it currently uses the most current version. The manufacturers introduced it in the year 2015, and since then, they have released lots of updates for its attributes and making changes for enhanced performance, productivity, and safety measures. To safeguard your device from malware, upgrade to the most recent version of the operating system. The updates come at zero cost and often download and install itself. If you are not using the most current version, you can also upgrade manually with the update assistant, media creation tool, which creates ways for easy installation.

Utilize antivirus

It is an essential component that every computer system should have so that it can quickly identify and remove malware before they do any damage to files and information or even crash the computer system. It is a software that you will install and always keep up to date with regular updates so that it can identify the most recent threats, which include worms, viruses, malicious codes, and lots more.

Windows Defender

OS 10 comes with an in-built Defender Antivirus that users can find in the defender security center and provides great protection to the computer system from viruses, trojans, and lots more. For additional protection, users can modify the protection level on the operating system.

Malwarebytes

Users that utilize the defender antivirus can also include this antivirus as another form of defense. It is a famous antivirus that can scan, identify, and eradicate the most potent virus or malware that wants to attack and infect the computer system. It a tool available at zero cost for users, and users can install it with another antivirus on devices running on OS 10. The tool also has a paid version that offers extra security for computer systems, can perform an extensive scan, and lots more.

Utilize anti-ransomware

It is a different type of malware that can keep users out of their systems by performing encryption on every file and ask you to for a certain sum before it unlocks your files without guarantee. You should be very careful with this one because releasing your files has no guarantee.

Utilize firewall

Another excellent way to safeguard your computer system from viruses and malware attacks is by utilizing a firewall. It is a hardware or software program that can block lots of attacks from viruses, malware, and hackers at large from infecting the computer system or steal a file from your computer through the cyberspace network and local network. There are lots of third-party tools for security which offers maximum security for networks. However, the OS 10 comes with an in-built and efficient firewall to protect the system which users will find enabled by default.

Chapter 6 – What is Cortana and how to use it

The feature is a practical help developed by Microsoft to help users search for any program on the operating system 10, and it can provide weather updates and other important information. The interesting feature disallows by default, but it is straightforward to turn it on and utilize.

Set up the feature on the OS 10

The feature is inside the taskbar, but before you begin:

Tap the start control key.

Tap all applications.

Select Cortana.

Tap the Cortana control key.

Select utilize Cortana.

Tap yes to turn on the inking, speech, and typing. The interesting feature gets to know the user more help the user's finish tasks. Tap no if you do not want the feature. Now feel free to type whatever you want and watch how interesting it can get.

Pin the feature to the taskbar

Although the attribute is within the taskbar, sometimes you may not find it there. If you do not want to open the feature application anytime you want to use it, you should pin it to the taskbar, and you save your precious time of searching for it.

Right-tap the taskbar

Tap Cortana.

Tap your desired option:

Hidden hides Cortana from the taskbar.

Show the feature logo will display the Cortana's circle logo within the taskbar.

"Show Search box" in the taskbar.

Turn the feature on

Tap Windows key + S together to launch the feature.

Tap the Notebook control key.

Tap Settings.

Toggle the On/Off switch

For instance, if you're searching for anything through the web, want to get scores of your favorite team, say, "Hey, Cortana," and speak.

Train the feature to reply to your voice only

Yes, you can do that. The amazing feature can reply to only your voice if you want it to, which means you are the only person that can use it. If you want that to happen, then you have to train the feature to understand your voice. Ensure that your environment is quiet before the training begins to avoid distractions. Use the following steps:

Tap Windows key + S simultaneously to launch the feature.

Tap the Notebook control key. You will find it below the house logo on your visual display.

Tap Settings.

Select to learn my voice.

Tap Start.

Now the feature will give you instructions to follow, like saying a particular word several times out loud. So be loud and clear, and the feature will recognize the voice and respond to only you.

Disable Cortana

When the OS 10 came to life, you can switch off Cortana by just toggling a button, but just turning that button off causes some problems for Windows search. However, switching it off now does not break search inn similar fashion, but it has its effect. It is not an easy task to turn the feature off now in

OS 10. The best way to turn the feature off in OS 10 is by utilizing the group policy. Still, the group policy editor is unavailable in the operating system home until you get it installed yourself. It is where you require the registry to make the changes, and it is a straightforward process. The exciting feature incorporates into the OS and Windows search. Therefore you will lose some Windows attributes when you disable the feature: reminders, news, and natural language go through your files.

Ensure that you type 'Regedit' in the search bar.

Utilize Windows key + R and input 'Regedit.' Both work fine.

Proceed to HKEY_LOCAL_MACHINE\SOFTWAR E\Policies\Microsoft\Windows\Windo ws Search.

Right-tap space and choose DWORD and new (32-bit) Value.

Give it a name, and you can name it 'AllowCortana' and 0 Value.

Tap OK.

You just disabled the feature, and it will not disturb you anymore. You will need a massive Windows update to enable the feature again if you need to utilize it in the future.

Chapter 7 – Fix Windows 10 problems

While you utilize OS 10, you can run into several types of problem, here are a few problems and how to solve them:

Glitch: Awkward software update reloads

Solution:

OS 10 is internet-based, and it is a bonus, but not every time. When your system has to restart during the process, that's where the frustration sets in. It happens mostly at unexpected times, which can lead to loss of work and be very inconvenient. The easiest way to fix this problem is by proceeding to settings, security, and update and tap Windows Update, select improved options, and update the schedule for restarting. That setting will make the OS ask for a reboot as an alternative to disrupting your work and losing vital information.

Glitch: Insufficient space for OS 10 installation

Solution:

Problems can arise from the installation process of OS 10. Your drive needs a particular free space because some elements need to function properly to install it. The required space is 16gigabytes. To see free space on your system proceeding to this PC, you will find the available space on your computer under each of your installed drives, or right-click and tap properties. It will give you a much-improved overview.

Glitch: Problems while changing wireless sense and privacy

Solution:

One important factor you should know is that data security is important, and you should be wary of hackers. Although the OS 10 has its in-built security measures that can protect your personal computer, you should not just rely on that. The first thing you should do is to switch off the wireless sense because it distributes your wireless passwords to every OS 10 computers on its account. To switch the feature off, proceed to start, tap settings and select internet and network, then wireless and click on manage wireless settings. Switch all options off.

Glitch: Problems updating old software to function properly

Solution:

Every version has problems of its own, and the OS 10 has its fair share. Migrating from OS 8.1 to 10 is not as frustrating as moving from 7 to 8, but some apps can break or not function anymore in the process. If any of your apps stop working, you should head into the store to search for updates, and if the problem remains unsolved, you should remove and reinstall the application. If that did not solve the problem as well, then you should search for other alternatives.

Glitch: Problems with printer compatibility

Solution

If you utilize an old device, issues with printers' compatibility will arise, and that can be a serious headache. If you migrate from OS 7 to 10, you should ensure that you update the drivers of your printers, which make them in an upgraded and good shape. It is a straightforward problem to solve, find your printer's name, and get all the recent compatible drivers of the OS 10. Ensure that you get the products from the original website of the manufacturers and follow directions to install them correctly and enjoy them.

Glitch: OS 10 back up issues

Solution:

One of the most unfortunate incidents that could ever happen to your personal computer is the loss of important information and finding out that you did not back your system up. To do that is a straightforward task to perform, proceed to settings > Security and updates, then back up. You can also back your information's on another drive as well as utilize other features.

Glitch: Touchpad tussle

Solution:

Laptops that come with touchpad is great for the OS 10, but there have been issues that the migration from OS 7 or 8 to 10 shatter it. The best way to solve that issue is to see if your keyboard has a button that switches the pad off. If that is not the case, proceed to devices, touchpad, and mouse, more options for the mouse. You will now see a new window, tap system settings, devices, and enable the pad. If these solutions solve the problem. Tap the Windows key + X, tap system manager, select mice, and pointing gadgets, then driver update. That should solve the problem.

Glitch: Browsers tussle

Solution:

OS 10 has a fantastic edge browser that replaces internet explorer. Lots of people continue to prefer the old browsers, so if you have a love for Firefox or chrome, you can revert your browser to your desired choice. To perform that task, launch edge, find a Windows 10 version of either and download. Install and set as default. Proceed to settings and tap default applications > web browser and choose your desired browser. Edge continues to improve anyway.

Glitch: Searching for safe mode

Solution:

It is a way of loading a personal computer and run the device without any startup applications and with just important drivers, which lets the system load successfully. In the OS 10, you can find the safe mode by holding the Shift key in the loading process.

Glitch: Let Windows know your location

Solution

There are lots of applications that show locations and function perfectly with the OS 10. You can update the site of your system by proceeding to start, tap settings, language and time, select language and region, and choose your country. To switch your location on, proceed to settings, tap privacy, location, and turn it on.

Glitch: Searching for files through tags

Solution:

If you are the type that has lots of files on your system and has issues frequently with finding one when you need it, you should find your files with tags in OS 10. If you want a file tagged, then right-click on the file and tap properties, proceed to details, select tags below description by typing it. Utilize those tags whenever you are looking for something. It is fast and reliable.

Glitch: Install applications downloaded from the internet

Solution:

The idea of getting an application from the internet instead of the store does not sit down well with OS 10; the way you install those types of application is not a straightforward process, unlike store applications. To install these applications, you need to tamper with Windows security settings. To perform this task, Proceed to the search box, find Windows defender, and go through its page. Select Settings, and you will see the functions of the defender. It is where you will perform the fine-tuning. Exclusions are the focus here. Select add exclusion to include the file you want to install, and the defender will not interfere.

Chapter 8 – Hidden features of Windows 10

Run as administrator in the Run window

Some applications need an elevated administrator access token to execute their exercises or functions. For instance, anytime a program, you want to run output denied or any form of error.

It displays the UAC message to get credentials which enable an app to utilize total administration access token in any of these occurrences:

The app will require the token access, and you can do that y utilizing a development concept called embedded manifest.

The UAC identifies the app as a setup app.

Right-click on the app and select Run as administrator when you want to launch a program.

Limit Internet bandwidth for downloading updates

To reduce the impact of your cyberspace network connection while updates are on, utilize delivery optimization to set a limit on the usage of the bandwidth on your computer system

Launch settings

Select security and updates

Select the link for advanced options.

Now you can check the limit of bandwidth that downloading pictures will use.

Determine your desired bandwidth with the slider.

Check the amount of bandwidth that

uploading updates to a different computer will use on the cyberspace network option.

Set the right bandwidth for uploads.

To set the right data limit on your gadget for each month, you can also view the upload limit for each month.

Set the limit for upload in gigabyte with the slider

However, you should know that the upload concepts will only function if you configure the deliver optimization to permit downloads from a different computer, utilizing the PCs on the cyberspace network and local network. If you wish to reduce the speed of the data, the devices use, use a computer on my local network.

Traffic restriction for cyberspace network connections

Utilize the Windows key + I control keys to launch the settings application.

Choose the internet and network.

Tap data usage. Below the segment for the overview, you will find the total amount of data that the device uses from the last thirty-days for ethernet links and wireless.

Select the link to see the usage details for every app on the system.

One benefit of the settings application is that you can see UWP apps as well as the data used for basic desktop apps.

Check the usage of data on the OS

OS 10 keep track of the traffic for every network adapter. Follow the below steps:

Launch settings

Select internet and network

Select data usage

View the data usage below the segment for the overview, and you will see the data used for the last thirty days.

Users can select check usage for each application to view which app utilizes more data.

Protection against ransomware viruses

It does not matter if you are using a new personal computer or the same old one you have been using for a long time ago, you should keep it secure. You can secure the device with the below steps:

Ensure that the computer has the most recent version of the operating system and up to date.

Enable the Windows security to safeguard the device from different malware and virus.

Enable file history

Ensure that you back the contents on the computer up more often.

Utilize the space for storage to make two copies of the computer information.

Several sections on a flash drive

Back the data inside the universal serial bus up and insert it into the port:

Now you should install the Lexar bootit program to move forward:

Mark the universal serial bus as removable:

Ensure that you open the disk management on Windows by right-clicking on My Computer and clicking manage.

It will delete the entire partition

Ensure that you create the new partition and complete the process.

Automatic clean install of the OS 10

If you run the OS 10 on your system, you can simply refresh the computer system if you want to reset it.

Select settings

Click on security and update

Select recovery and tap get started.

Tap the remove everything button. You can decide to keep certain files, and the gadget will keep it.

It will display remove all the files and clean the drive. You can decide to reset and keep a few pieces of information or reset to format the entire system, which can take a few minutes to complete.

After selecting your desired option, tap the reset control key, and that's all. The system then reloads after a few minutes, depending on the device speed. When it completes, the OS will be completely new.

Windows 10 game mode

users can now force game modes in certain games either tested by the manufacturing company or not. The location of the game mode toggle has changed in the most recent version of the OS. To perform that task now, utilize the OS settings menu.

launch the settings menu

Tap the gaming segment

Scroll to the game mode segment

Tap to turn the mode off or on.

Shortcuts on the left side of the Start menu

Begin by selecting the start and launch settings. Proceed to personalization, select start. Go to the options that display the most used apps and displays newly included applications. It will leave a hole on the start menu left side. Proceed again to personalization, select start, and click on the folder that displays on start. It is only the folder that can display on the left.

Console Login

Users have few ways to enable administrative profiles in OS 10. Follow the below method to perform the task.

Proceed to run —> control and input userpasswords2

Select advanced button beneath the user management

Right-click on admin user and select Properties

Uncheck the mark on disable account and tap okay.

Allow the admin profile

Users should always safeguard the admin profile pass-key by creating a new pass-key. The admin account comes without a password.

When you authorize the profile, it displays users on the login visual display. Select the username and input the pass-key to gain access as an admin into your personal computer.

Secret Dark Theme

The OS comes with a very slick interface, but users may not like bright colors because it can be tough on their eyes. Users now have the choice to use a dark theme for lots of applications by tweaking them a little.

Tap the Windows and R together to launch a run dialog, input the words (Regedit), and hit enter.

Proceed   to   the

HKEY_LOCAL_MACHINE and select software, click on Microsoft and select the current version, tap themes, and then personalize.

If you cannot find the folder, right-click on themes and tap new and then select key. You can now rename it.

Right-click on personalizing and choose new, select the value DWORD (32-bit). You can give it a name that reads AppsUseLightTheme with a value of 0.

Go through the process again to log out of the account.

Screen video recording

The OS comes with an in-built recorder on the screen that users can utilize without the need for new things. To perform that task, follow the below methods:

The first thing to do is to tap the Windows key and the G key together and select yes, it's a game.

Right from that moment, the recording becomes an easy task. Utilize the red control key to control the recording, and you can use it to stop and start the record or utilize settings to create an automatic time for cut off on the record.

When you are done with that, it will save the file in MP4 format inside the capture or videos folder.

Laptop touchpad gestures

The touchpad gestures function with devices with pads with accuracy, below are few gestures that users can utilize on their computers:

Click: You can carry out a click by simply touching the touchpad. You do not need to click or press a button to perform that function.

Right-click: If the right-click is the action you want to perform instead of a left-click, perform a tap twice on the tap in quick succession. You can also use one finger by tapping in the lower section of the pad.

Drop and Drag: If you want to drag an item — You have to perform this function the same way you use a mouse, tap, and use the other hand to move the item to your desired location. Release the holding when you get to the position.

Scroll: If you want to dance through a web page, files or anything else on the computer, utilize the scroll wheel, place two of your fingers on the pad and move vertically or horizontally, it should be based on what you want.

Zoom: To either zoom out and in, Put two of your fingers on the pad and give them a little stretch the same way you zoon on a touchscreen.

Open Task View: Put three of your fingers on the pad and take a swipe upward. Use the mouse cursor to click on the pad if you want to switch back to it. Use the same three fingers swipe to exit the task view without clicking a window.

Remote access to any files on the computer

Tap the Windows and X keys and click on settings to launch Windows settings.

Tap system option

Tap the option for remote desktop

Toggle on the allow remote desktop

Click on yes.

Now you should authorize select users that can gain remote access to the computer beneath the user account segment.

You will see a list of users on the computer at that moment who have access to use the remote desktop.

If your profile is not on the list, select the add key and input your account to get on the list. Select okay when you finish, and your account will not have the authorization to use the remote desktop and access files as well as manage files and transfer them on the same local network.

Or you can close it by tapping the cancel control key if you do not want to include your account.

Command-line shortcuts

You will find shortcuts turned off in the most recent version of the OS 10 by default. Check by launching the command prompt, click on the start button and select all apps, tap Windows system, and click on command prompt. Now right-click on the prompt title bar.

Select properties to launch a new window, check the box right next to allow control key shortcuts, tap okay so that the changes will take effect.

To copy text that you select to the clipboard: Control + C

To paste the text: Control + V

Enable and disable hotkeys in OS 10

To enable hotkeys, you need to launch the command prompt

Input (explorer shell: AppsFolder) at the prompt and select enter.

Now, right-click on any application and create a shortcut.

Tap yes

Right-click on the logo and tap properties.

To turn it off, tap the Windows and the X key, then select U and tap U again.

To restart, tap the Windows and X key, then select U and then R.

Screenshot timer in the Scissors application

To perform this task, you need the snipping tool. You need to launch the tool and select the delay. Then choose your desired delay time. It can be from 0 to five seconds, for instance.

Click on the arrow right beside (new) and select a snip mode from its list of options.

Then, proceed to the menu that you will capture in five seconds when it reaches that time, the screen freezes and dims a little, and then captures the menu in whichever form you select.

When the screenshot loads into the editor for images, modify it whichever way you want and tap save to keep the image on your computer.

Built-in PDF printer

The first thing to do is to launch any document or web page.

After loading, select the app menu. Choose the file and then select print.

Users can also utilize the control and p key to perform the same function.

There will be a pop-up of the print dialog.

Select the name of the printer and choose how to print in pdf format within the available options.

Choose the pages to print and select the prink key.

It will tell you to store the doc/page and give it a name before you save it in pdf format.

Wait until it completes the process, and you can have your file in your preferred format.

You should utilize an application that works with the print function properly. Whenever you print a document, ensure that you also select a layout that supports pdf so that the result can be readable.

Built-in support for MKV, FLAC, and HEVC

Support for Free Lossless Audio Codec audio files

It is a format that lots of audiophiles use. It combines different types of the file by providing top-notch audio using the file tags for ID3 music. It means that you are losing audio value, compressed, but with the omission of low audio data omissions that disturbs mp3 listeners and so on. It has metadata tags that you can use to sort different music collections from genres, to artists, and so on.

Playing files in this format is an excellent choice for music lovers. The files now display in explorers as the new G logo and play inside the groove player by default.

Support for HEVC

It is the standard that functions in the position of the 4K video, and it provides much more resolution reaching 1080p, which you cannot find in several traditional HDTV televisions. If you want to watch or edit a video from the most recent 4k, enable device now, or at a later date, the high-efficiency video coding has the support of the OS 10 and make tasks easy to perform from the beginning.

Support for MKV video

The news that users can now play files in Matroska video format in Windows came as great excitement for users that have an extensive collection of movies that are in the video container format. The file displays like a basic video file having the blue board logo, and when you double click on the logo, it will display the most recent movies and television player.

Scrolling inactive window contents on the OS

If you want to stop scrolling background Windows any time you decide to hover in the OS 10.

Go to your start menu and launch settings

Select devices in the categories.

Select the mouse page.

Turn off the inactive Windows anytime I hover across.

Upgraded from Windows 7 - Win + X menu

To utilize this menu editor, you can add applications to the menu in the OS 10. For instance, this is an example of adding UAC settings to it. Follow the below method to perform the task:

Tap add a program, and there will be a list drop-down, choose to add a program.

When the file dialog launches, select the below code:

(C:\Windows\System32\UserAccountC ontrolSettings.exe)

The app demands the item name to include, input the name, and select restart explorer if you want the newly added items to display in the menu.

Launch the menu, and there will be new settings that you can use instantly.

Use presets

Users can now utilize a few presets that are available. Beneath the include a program, and include paint, services, and few in-built desired items. Ensure that you select the reload explorer so that the items you add can be visible. Apart from presets and custom applications, users can also include items in the control panel as well as tools in the administrative section to the menu. Utilize the correct instructions to add a program, also to add administrative and other items. Add an item to include an item from anywhere, for instance.

Eradicate the items on the Win+X menu

The menu editor gives users the ability to delete items that they predefine through the menu. For instance, If you find any item on the menu that you do not want there, you can remove it or replace it. To remove them, follow the below process:

Click on the item and select the remove control key.

Select reload explorer, and the changes that you made on an item will take effect.

To-Do List Sharing

Here, users can develop a link to lists that they send through the one drive cloud storage. It lets the receiver remove or add items to the same list on the same drive, similar to the way you collaborate spreadsheets while using Google Docs. In the version for web, right-click on the list you created and tap share list if you wish to send the file around. The sender has the power to lock the list if they feel comfortable with the changes.

Because the cloud is where to-do lists stores instead of being on your computer only, users can build a list on an OS 10 personal computer and then share or watch them on a mobile phone compatible with the application at a later date. The manufacturing company also included the feature users can use to hide lists after they create them and organize them in different formats like date or alphabetical order.

Minimize all Windows except active

You can now close every window at once, unlike the traditional closing of Windows one after another. However, users can also close all Windows and leave the active window open. Below are a few methods to perform that task:

Minimize through the Windows and D shortcut

Tap the Windows and D key together, and it will minimize every window that you may have opened at once. If you want to restore the Windows, tap the Windows and D key again. If you want every window to minimize except the active one, tap the Windows title bar and hold the left control key on the mouse down and shake it. Move the title bar to the left and then to the right quickly.

Utilize show desktop control key

The desktop control key is a small section on the Windows taskbar. Tapping the control key displays the desktop instantly and also open every minimized window. Whenever you tap the control key again, it restores your Windows to your visual display.

Utilizing Windows Taskbar

Right-click on an area that contains no information within the taskbar and chooses display desktop, It minimizes every window and displays the desktop. To restore the Windows to their initial position, right-click again and tap the display Windows option.

Quick access to Properties

Going through the properties dialog box of any folder or file in the OS 10 is a straightforward task to perform. Below are a few steps to perform that task.

Launch Windows explorer and expand the ribbon menu, although you could find it in an expanded form. But if it is not, tap the arrow that drops down or utilize the control and F1 shortcut on the keyboard.

Or

Proceed to the folder that owns the property you wish to access and select the folder. Go to the ribbon menu that you expanded and select the control key with the name properties. Whenever you tap that button, the folder's properties will come up. The method functions across all the operating systems and not limited to the most recent versions. It is a convenient, fast, and straightforward method.

Quick navigation in the Start menu

Select a file or folder that you do not want on your device with your finger and hold it down, there will be a pop-up option with unpinning, select it, and it will remove the selected file or folder.

You can now begin to add different items of your choice. Adding items to the start menu makes it easy to reach whenever its time to use the applications.

Follow the below steps to attach applications or programs to the start menu:

Select start and tap all applications.

The menu presents a list in alphabetical order of every program or apps installed on the device. Right-click on the program that you want to move to the menu and select pin to start. Continue to repeat the task until you add every program or app to the start menu.

Users need to right-click and pin every item one after the other.

However, you should know that the menu tiles have no limitations to the programs and applications. When you get to the desktop environment, right-click on the folder, program, file, or any item you want to pin to the menu and tap pin to start from the menu that pops up.

Starting a new instance of the program

Users can now authorize or attach new startup programs in the OS 10 by returning to the task manager section.

Now, right-click on start and tap task manager when the option pops up.

When you get to that section, tap the startup tab, and right-click on the app, you want to attach the startup too and enable.

Virtual desktop

Adding virtual desktops is an easy task

to perform. Select the task view control key. If you cannot find the control key, then it is most likely off. Right-click on a free space while on the taskbar and select display task view. Users can also launch the task view controls by tapping the Windows and tab key shortcuts through the keyboard.

The view is a complete display application switcher that displays every application that runs on the personal computer. Users can switch easily to any application by tapping it. If you have been worried about setting up more virtual desktop, well, you only need your task view shows to perform that function. To attach a new desktop, select a new desktop below the visual display.

The operating system lets users create lots of desktops as possible. There is no limitation to the number of desktops that you can create, and users can now create according to their needs, which is a wonderful and exciting attribute on the most recent version of the OS. The number of created desktops depends on your workload and how much organizing you require.

Navigate through virtual desktops

Whenever you have above one desktop, the task view will display every desktop at the visual display bottom. Utilizing a mouse to hover across a desktop displays the active window. You can select a particular window to jump to another and make the new one the focus. It is the same way users switch applications on one desktop. It only requires better organization and different virtual workspaces. Users can also switch it through the use of the keyboard by tapping the Windows and tab key to launch the task view and let go of both keys. Now, select the tab key again to transfer what you select to the desktop row. Now, utilize the arrow keys to navigate through desktops and choose enter to move to the desktop that you select.

Users can also navigate through desktops without the use of the task view. You should click on the Windows, control, and right or left keys together. And if the device that you have has a touch visual display, you should swipe with four fingers.

Conclusion

This book contains several vital information about Windows 10. The concepts in this book give users a good understanding and excellent usage of the OS 10. It's an extensive introduction, setting it up and how to use the OS, what you need to know before you switch from different versions of Windows, how to protect your personal computer, Cortana and how to utilize the feature, and the best programs to use on the operating system. You will get explanations on fixing common problems users face and then complete the book with its hidden features, and they include screen video recording, scrolling inactive window contents.

I hope, that you really enjoyed reading my book.

Thanks for buying the book anyway!

Printed in Great Britain
by Amazon